Dedicated to my husband and our two daughters.

I am so grateful to share with you a wonderful life filled
with so much love, laughter, and art.
Thank you from the bottom of my heart for your patience
while I follow my dreams.
Your endless support and inspiration mean the
world to me. You are my everything and I love you.

The BRAVEST WORRIER

Written and Illustrated by: Angelique Monet

5th WONDER PUBLISHING

Sometimes I **WORRY**, and then I **WORRY** about **WORRYING** so much!

I **WORRY** about small things, and big things, and wide things, and such!

I really can't help it you see!

I'm the **WORRIEST WORRIER** as a **WORRIER** can be!

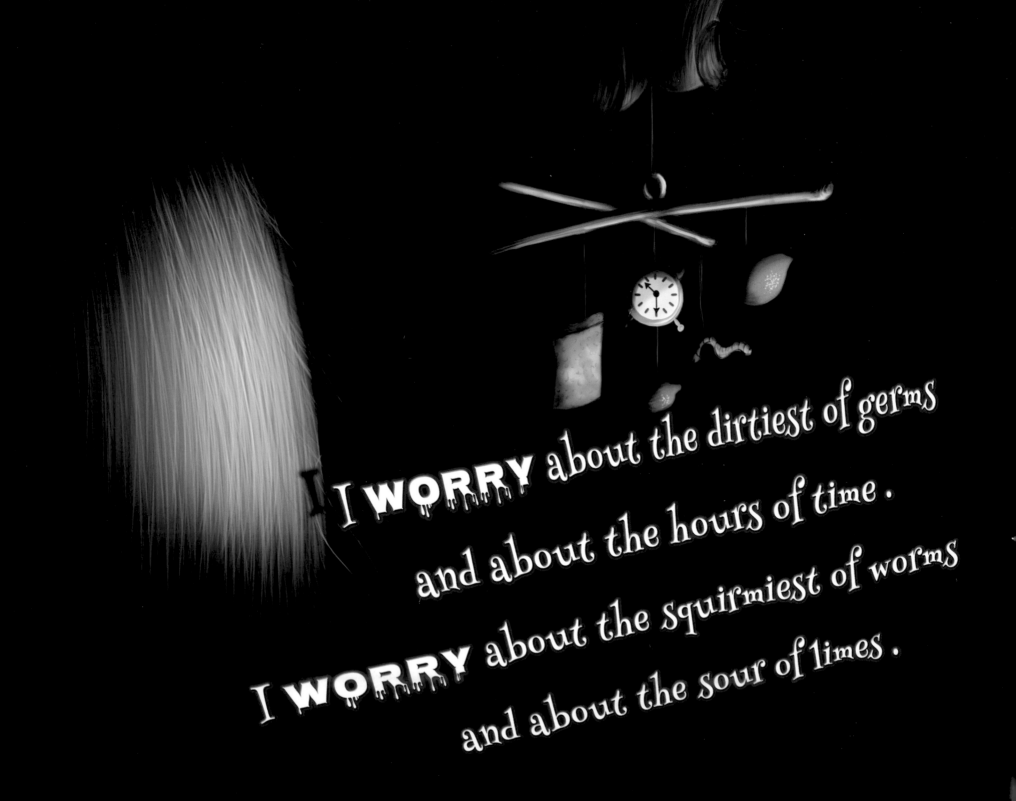

I **WORRY** about the dirtiest of germs
and about the hours of time.

I **WORRY** about the squirmiest of worms
and about the sour of limes.

I **WORRY** about eating the wrong and forgetting the right.

I **WORRY** about dreams that I haven't even had sleeping tonight.

I
WORRY
about
the
rain
and
the
Lightning
it throws!

I **WORRY** about the paint and ink on my hands!

Even
though
I wash
and
scrub
as
hard
as
I
can!

I worry about my tummy and the twists that it feels

when I

WORRY

about the monsters who I know aren't real.

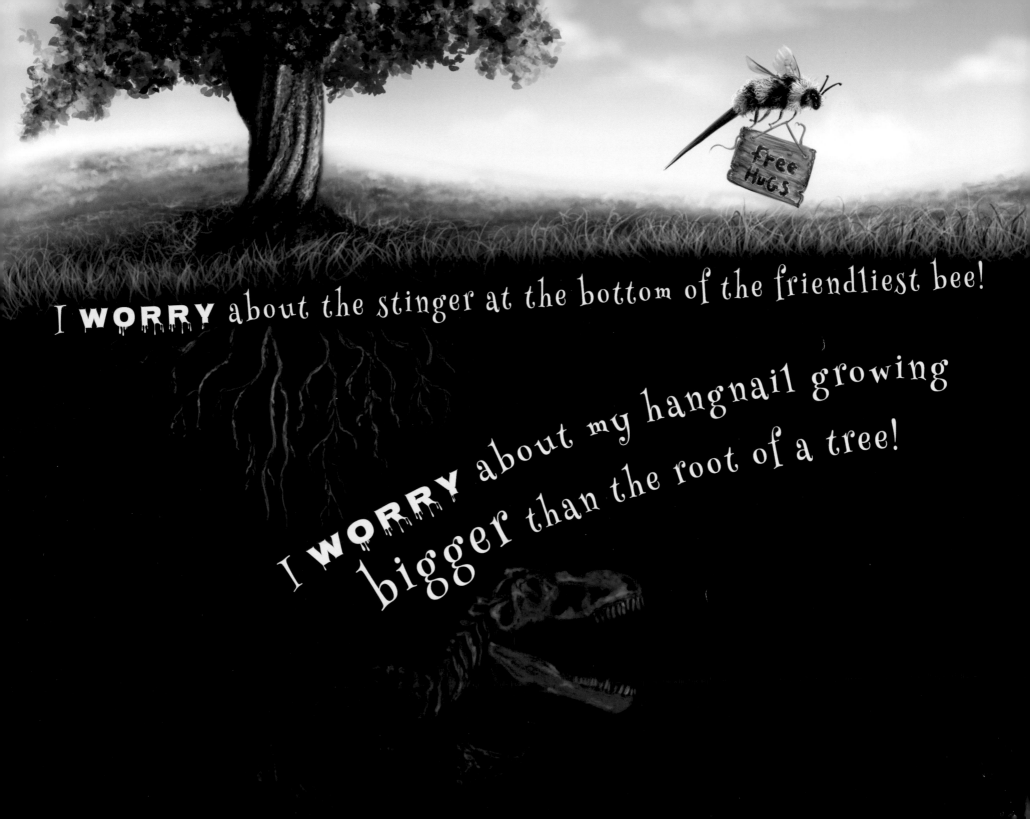

I **WORRY** about the stinger at the bottom of the friendliest bee!

I **WORRY** about my hangnail growing bigger than the root of a tree!

I **WORRY** about that hole Swallowing me!

WORRY Family Reunion 1973

I **WORRY** about the smelliest of smells and the dirtiest of dirt.

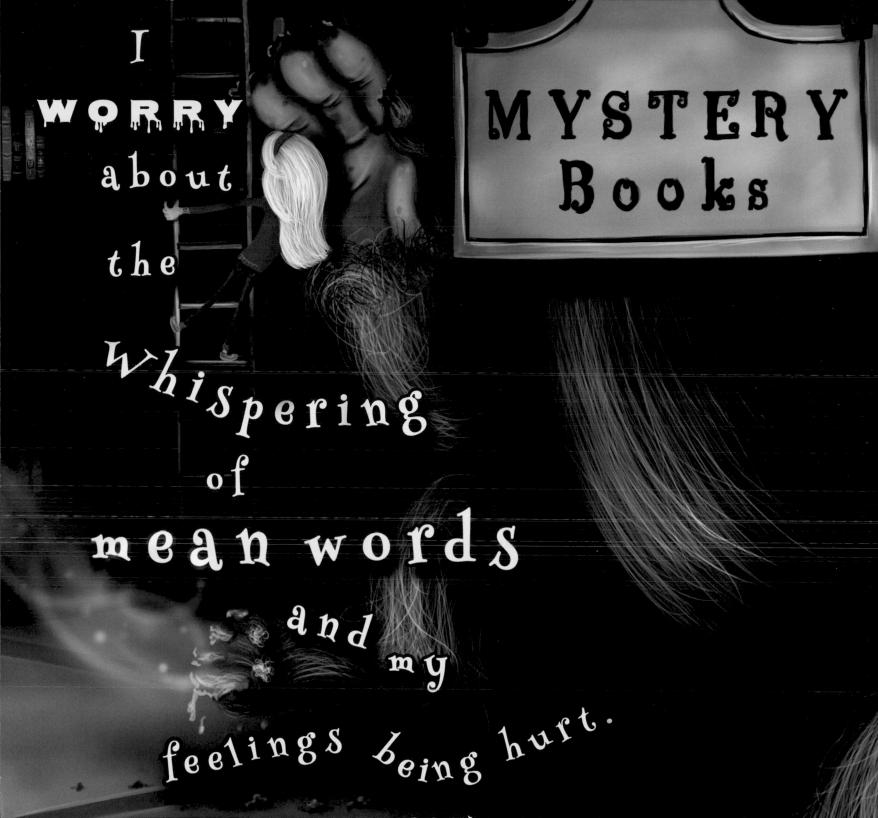

I **WORRY** about the whispering of **mean words** and my feelings being hurt.

MYSTERY Books

I **WORRY** about not knowing

the most of all I should know!

I **WORRY** about not

going to the ends of the farthest I should go!

Oh the **WORRYING** a **WORRIER** could do
Could quickly turn a new **WORRY** into two!
Really! I mean it! I **WORRY** enough
for both **me** and **you**!

Oh it's
hopeless you
see!
WORRY has
gotten

the best
of me.

Oh the

I wish to leave behind.

The wheels in my mind are really turning!

Brewing up some new

WORRIES

I feel them burning!

WORRY
Begone

BLOW
Worries
AWAY

$1,000,000

SUDDENLY
SAD

You're heavy **WORRY!** My back aches and my muscles are really quite sore! You take up too much space Crowding and Pushing from ceiling to Floor!

♥WORRY

All this **WORRYING** has really got me thinking... and thinking, and thinking some more.

I've turned all the possibilities of fun into an incredible forgettable

BORE!

Get out of my thoughts
and out of my head!

Out of my dreams
and from under my bed!

Get out of my fun
and out of my play!

Get out of my life
and out of my way!

I will not **WORRY** about the fall from a tree,
Or a scratch on my knee,
Not even the sting from the hugest of bees,
Because none of these things have happened to me.

Not a thunder clap, Or some sticky sap,
Not even the pain from a static zap,
Will make me run to my momma's lap.

Not another moment will I give

RoARRR

to the **WORRY** that won't let me live

this wild adventure I get once as a kid.

I realized through all the ups and downs,
and a whole lot of tries,
That **WORRY** was nothing more than a
BULLY
carrying a big barrel of lies!
When I abandoned **WORRY**
Happiness
was the prize!

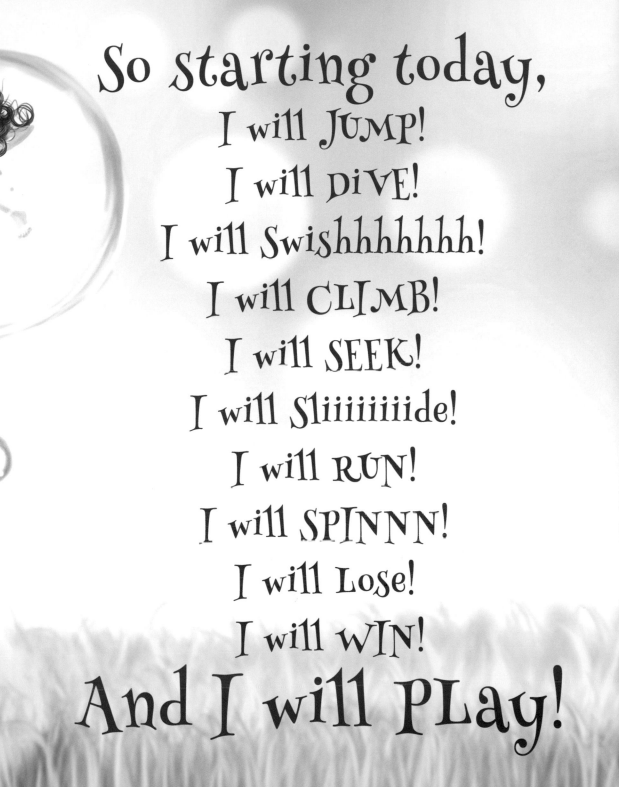

So starting today,
I will JUMP!
I will DIVE!
I will Swishhhhhhh!
I will CLIMB!
I will SEEK!
I will Sliiiiiiiide!
I will RUN!
I will SPINNN!
I will Lose!
I will WIN!
And I will PLay!

Bearing the courage to climb to the tippy tops of the highest of highs.

Arms wide open, leaping forward,
I am ready to fly!

Printed in Canada
First Edition - July 2016

Chief Editor Zawdie Little

Library of Congress Control Number: 2016910757

ISBN 978-0-692-74919-7

Fifth Wonder Publishing is a division of Fifth Wonder, LLC.
The Fifth Wonder Publishing name and logo are trademarks of Fifth Wonder, LLC.

Fifth Wonder Publishing
2221 Peachtree Road NE, Suite D208, Atlanta, GA 30309
www.fifthwonderpublishing.com

www.thebravestworrier.com